SCHIRMER'S LIBRARY
OF MUSICAL CLASSICS

Vol. 2108

CARL CZERNY

Collected Studies

The School of Velocity, Op. 299
The Art of Finger Dexterity, Op. 740
Thirty New Studies in Technics, Op. 849

ISBN 978-1-4950-0426-1

G. SCHIRMER, Inc.

DISTRIBUTED BY

HAL•LEONARD®
CORPORATION
7777 W. BLUEMOUND RD. P.O. BOX 13819 MILWAUKEE, WI 53213

www.musicsalesclassical.com
www.halleonard.com

CONTENTS

(continued on next page)

CARL CZERNY was born in Vienna, February 21, 1791. From Wenzel Czerny, his father, a Bohemian by birth, he inherited the Bohemian accent that marked his speech for life; and from his father he received pianoforte lessons almost as soon as he could move his fingers. He played little pieces when he was four years old, and at the age of fourteen he gave lessons. In 1800, according to Eiserle he played in public the C minor concerto of Mozart. His father and Wenzel Krumpholz took him to see Beethoven, one winter-day of that same year. There was a group of men in an untidy room of a house in the "Tiefen Graben." One of the group had shaggy, pitch-black hair, which stood on end; he

wore a beard of a week's growth; his rough clothes, of a hairy stuff, made the boy think of Robinson Crusoe. This man was Beethoven, who then heard Carl play Mozart's C major concerto and the "*sonate pathétique.*" He said to Wenzel Czerny, the modest musician, "your son has great talent. I will be his teacher. Send him here twice a week, and let him bring Philipp Emanuel Bach's 'True Method of playing the Clavier.'" Thus began the instruction which lasted until Carl was fourteen years old. In a written certificate Beethoven spoke of his "extraordinary progress and remarkable memory." He sent his nephew Karl to him for the study of the pianoforte; he intrusted him with the arrangement of "Leonore" for the pianoforte, and with other important work. In 1806 Czerny played Beethoven's C major concerto in public; in 1812 he was the pianist when the noble concerto in E flat was heard for the first time and Theodor Körner recorded the fact that it was a failure; and during the years 1818, 1819 and 1820 he gave recitals at his lodgings every Sunday from 11 till 1 o'clock, which were devoted to the pianoforte compositions of his master, and to which all lovers of music were welcome. But teaching and composition soon absorbed his time. It is said that his playing in his youth was characterized by brilliancy, and Fétis states that if Czerny had devoted himself solely to concert work he would have been one of the first of virtuosos; and others, among them Hanslick, say that his performance was without any display of artistic fire. With the exception of short trips to Leipzig, Paris, London and other towns, he passed his life in Vienna. He taught for ten or twelve hours a day until about twelve years before his death; and these last years were spent in composition and in the arranging of the works of others. His health failed him in 1854, and he was loath to leave his rooms. A gouty swelling first attacked his arm, which was encased in plaster. He composed although the disease spread. His last works, an *offertorium* and a sonata, were written fourteen days before his death, which took place July 15, 1857.

Czerny was small and frail. He was unassuming and amiable in company. He preferred to seclude himself, for he was a man of incredible industry. Music was to him "his only joy, his only occupation, his daily duty and his highest ideal." Until his sickness mastered him, the little man with golden spectacles and a large, round snuff-box was to be seen at noon in Diabelli's music-shop, where he would converse affably. His habits were simple; his life and speech were of uncommon purity. He was not without literary tastes, and a comedy, two dramas and verses by him are in the archives of the "Gesellschaft der Musikfreunde," in Vienna. He was accused, but undoubtedly with gross injustice, of avarice. His kindly deeds were remembered by many. He left a fortune of 100,000 florins. As he was never married and was without kin, he willed the money, with the exception of trifling legacies, to charitable institutions.

He was as fortunate in his pupils as they were in their master. Among the most celebrated were Emilie Belleville-Oury (1808-1880); Theodor Döhler (1814-1856); Theodor Kullak (1818-1882); and Franz Liszt (1811-1886). Although the instruction that Czerny received from Beethoven was irregular, it was the foundation of his own teaching. "In the first lessons," said Czerny, "Beethoven busied himself exclusively with the scales in all the keys. He showed me things that were then unknown to most players: the true position of the hands and the fingers, and the use of the thumb. I learned the full value of these rules only in later years. He was very particular about the legato." We are told of Czerny's course with Liszt, who in 1821, as an infant prodigy, so won the sympathy of the teacher that he taught him for a year and a half without reward of money, and loved him as a brother. He insisted on "a well-exercised touch and correct execution in moderate time. He taught, in his usual systematic manner, artistic technique and correctness of rendering." Yet it would be wrong to assume that he was merely a master of technique, when such an authority as Brahms declares, in referring to his editions of certain works of Bach and Scarlatti, that "we cannot to-day estimate Czerny's value too highly."

As a composer, he was first of all a marvel of fertility. Not without reason has he been called the Lope de la Vega of the pianoforte. His works are over 1,000 in number, and many of them embrace 50 or more pieces. The masses, oratorios, overtures, motets, concertos, symphonies, etc., have not withstood the ravages of Time. Czerny studied composition by reading the treatises of Türk, Kirnberger, Albrechtsberger, and Marpurg, and putting together the voice-parts of the quartets and the symphonies of Haydn and Mozart. He was skilled in composition, but he had little imagination, and hardly any originality.

His enduring monument is the series of studies for the education of youth, and for varied technical purposes. So ready was he in composition that he invented at once exercises for the needs of his pupils, suiting the peculiar want of each. About 1810 he began to publish studies for the use of students, the surpassing merit of which has been gratefully acknowledged by the virtuosos, the pedagogues, and the critics of all countries. For Czerny knew best of all (to borrow an idea from Hugo Riemann) how to expose clearly the necessary and natural form-foundations on which the structure of pianoforte-music rests. He also had the gift of leading the pupil step by step; and no detail in the art of pianoforte-playing escaped his observation.

— Philip Hale

THE SCHOOL OF VELOCITY
Op. 299, Book 1

Revised and fingered by
Max Vogrich

Carl Czerny
(1791–1857)

7

14

Molto Allegro. (ϕ = 104)

7.

p leggiermente non legato.

18

22

23

THE SCHOOL OF VELOCITY

Op. 299, Book 2

Revised and fingered by
Max Vogrich

Carl Czerny
(1791–1857)

11.

30

12.

Molto vivo e velocissimo. ($\bullet$ = 116)

14.

Molto Allegro. (♩ = 120)

18.

48

Molto vivace. ($\dot{\downarrow}$ = 63)

20.

THE SCHOOL OF VELOCITY
Op. 299, Book 3

Revised and fingered by
Max Vogrich

Carl Czerny
(1791–1857)

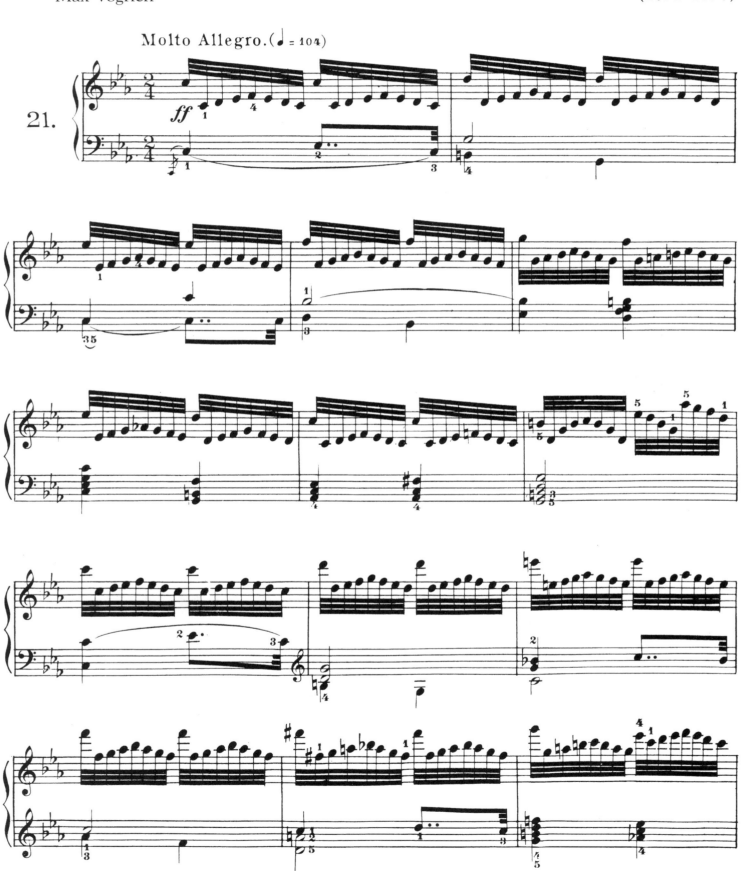

Molto Allegro. ($\flat$.=63)

23.

60

64

66

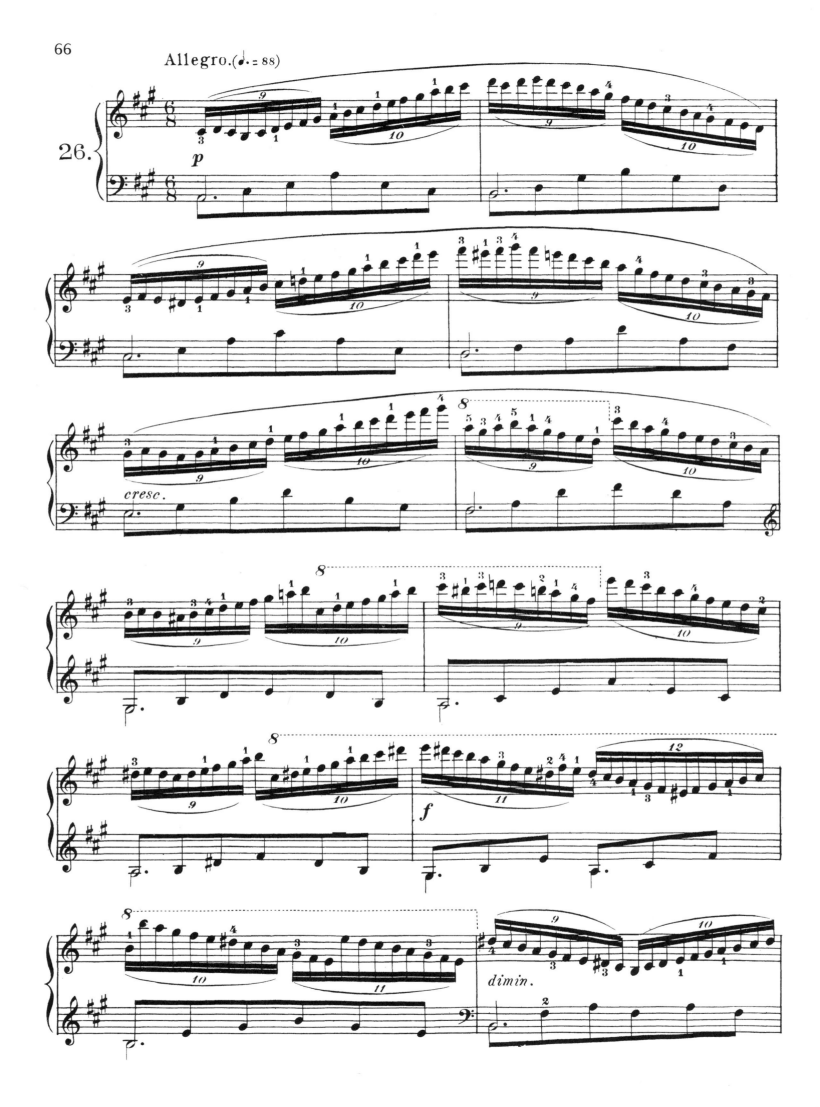

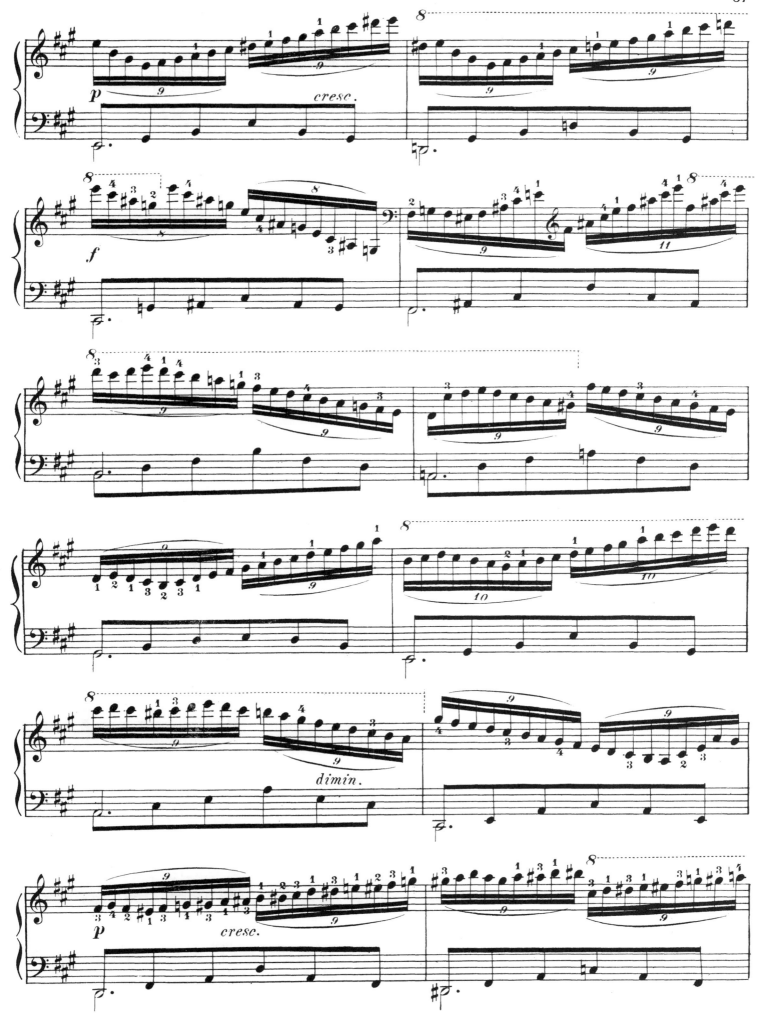

68

74

THE SCHOOL OF VELOCITY
Op. 299, Book 4

Revised and fingered by
Max Vogrich

Carl Czerny
(1791–1857)

Presto volante. ($\downharpoonleft$ = 100.)

32.

84

Allegro molto vivo ed energico. (♩= 88.)

34.

Allegro vivacissimo. (♩. = 108.)

35.

Presto. (♩ = 88.)

36.

Molto Allegro e giocoso. (♩ = 96.)

37.

Molto Allegro, quasi presto. (♩ = 84.)

38.

Presto. (à la Galopade.)($\bullet$ = 104.)

39.

THE ART OF FINGER DEXTERITY
Op. 740, Book 1

Revised and fingered by
Max Vogrich

1.

Carl Czerny
(1791–1857)

Action of the Fingers, the Hand quiet.

2.

The Passing under of the Thumb.

3.

Clearness in Rapidity.

4.

Light Motion in quiet Staccato.

5.

Evenness in double Passages.

Molto Allegro. ($\bullet$ = 84.)

124

6.

Clearness in broken Chords.

7

Changing the Fingers on one and the same Key.

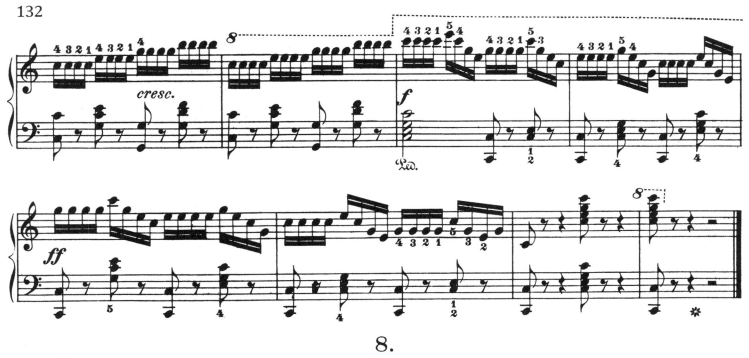

8.

Light Action of the Left Hand.

THE ART OF FINGER DEXTERITY

Op. 740, Book 2

Revised and fingered by
Max Vogrich

9.

Carl Czerny
(1791–1857)

Delicate Skips and Detached Notes.

139

10

Exercise in Thirds

11.

Readiness in changing the Fingers

12.

Flexibility of the Left Hand.

13.

The utmost Velocity.

14.

Chord-Passages.

15.
Extension, with great Strength.

Allegro agitato energico.($\bullet$=88.)

16.
Changing the Fingers in rapid Playing.

THE ART OF FINGER DEXTERITY
Op. 740, Book 3

Revised and fingered by
Max Vogrich

Carl Czerny
(1791–1857)

17.
Minor-scales in rapid tempo.

170

18.
Crossing the Hands quietly and with delicate Touch.

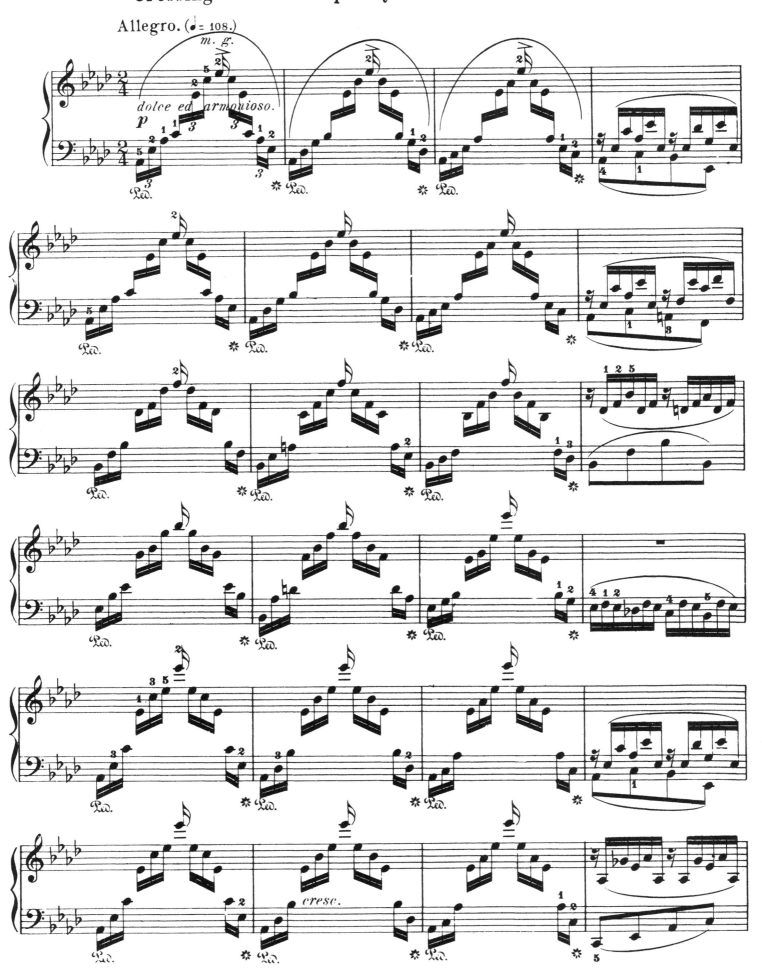

174

19.

Extension, the Hand quiet.

20.

Double Octaves.

21.

The same Movement in each Hand.

Molto Allegro. ($\quad$ = 80.)

22.

Trill-Study.

Molto Allegro. (♩=88.)

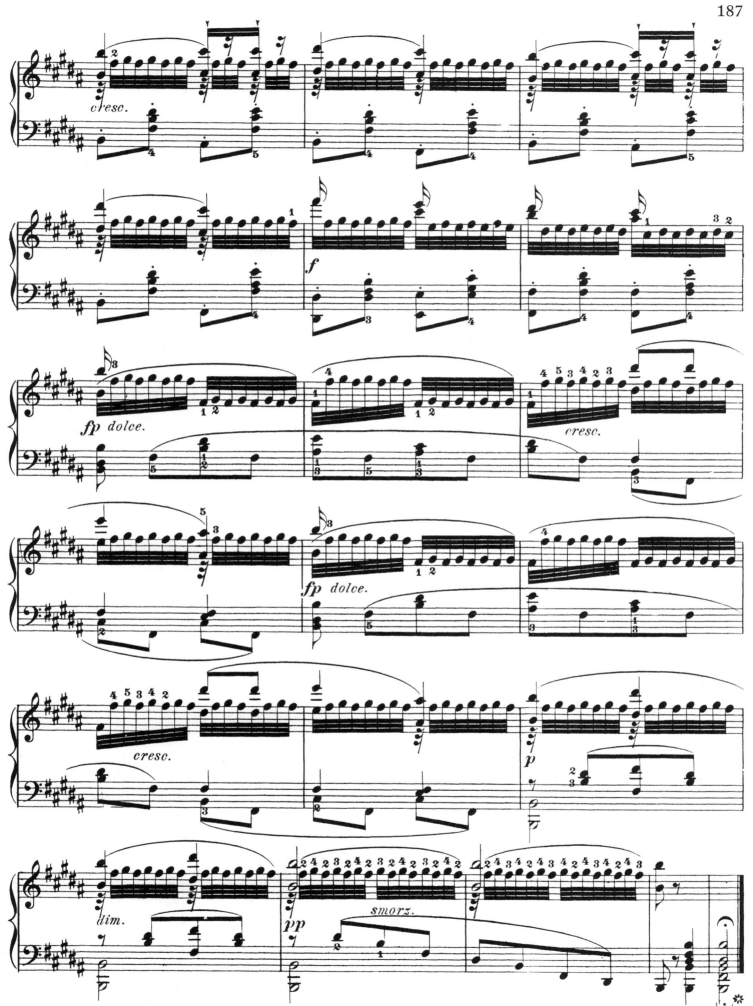

23.

Light-Touch in the Fingers of the Left Hand.

24.

The Thumb on the Black Keys, the Position of the Hand perfectly quiet.

Molto vivace con velocita. ($\flat$=110.)

195

THE ART OF FINGER DEXERITY
Op. 740, Book 4

Revised and fingered by
Max Vogrich

Carl Czerny
(1791–1857)

25.

Clearness in running Passages.

Molto Allegro. (♩ = 88)

26.

The utmost Velocity in Chord-Passages.

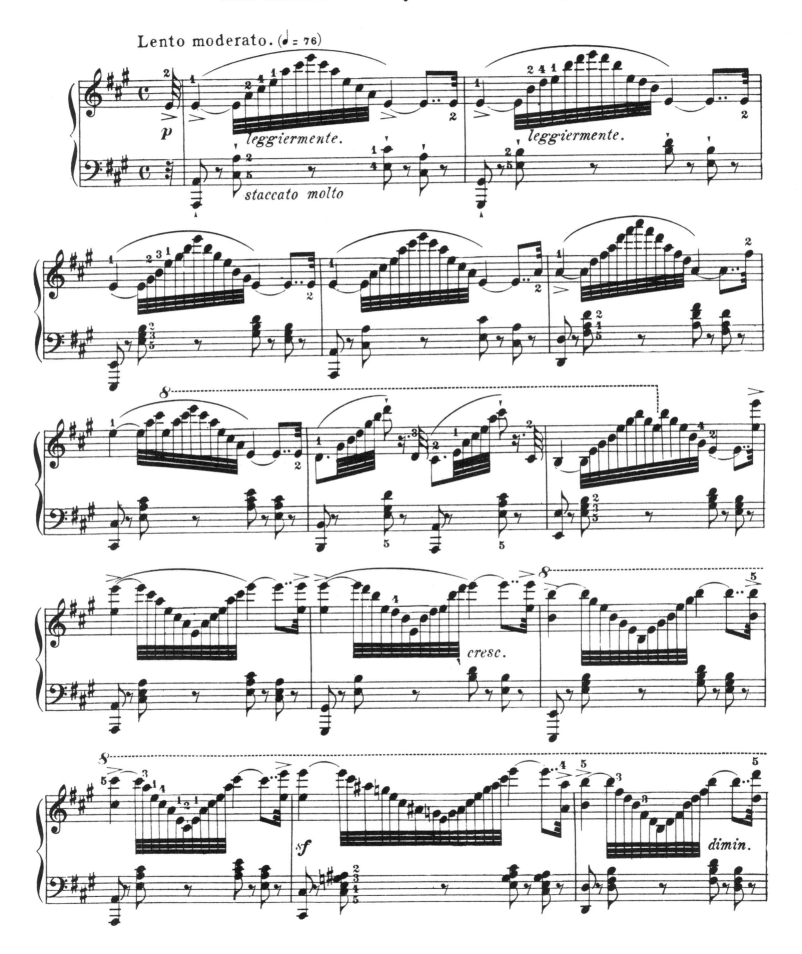

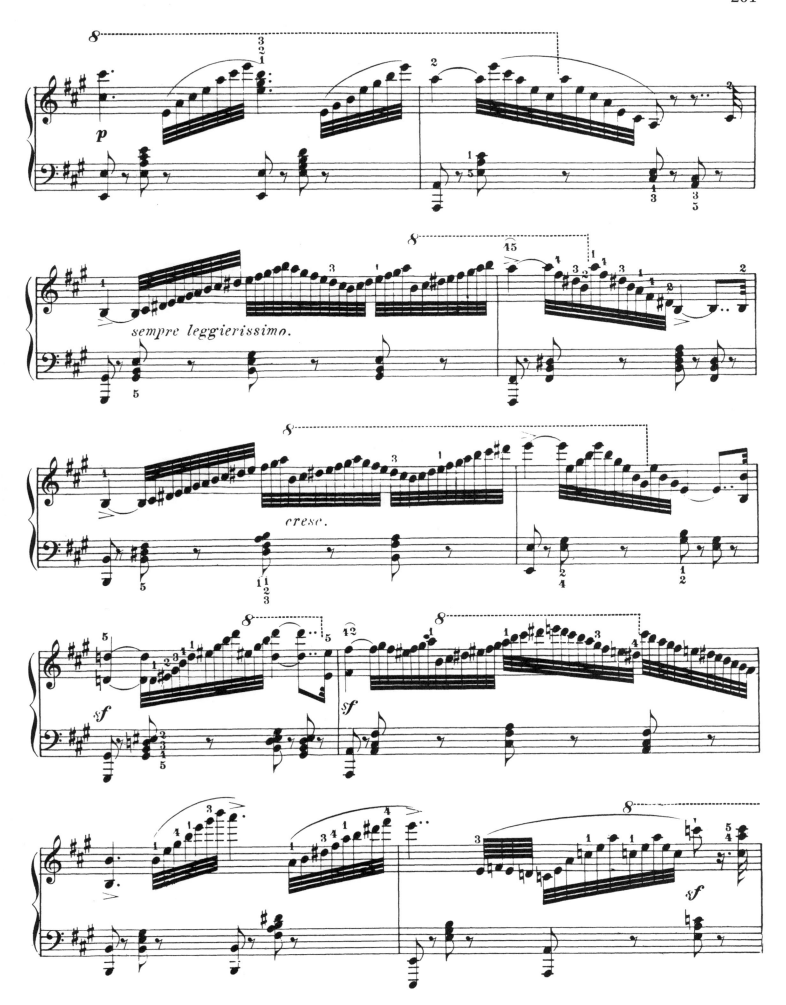

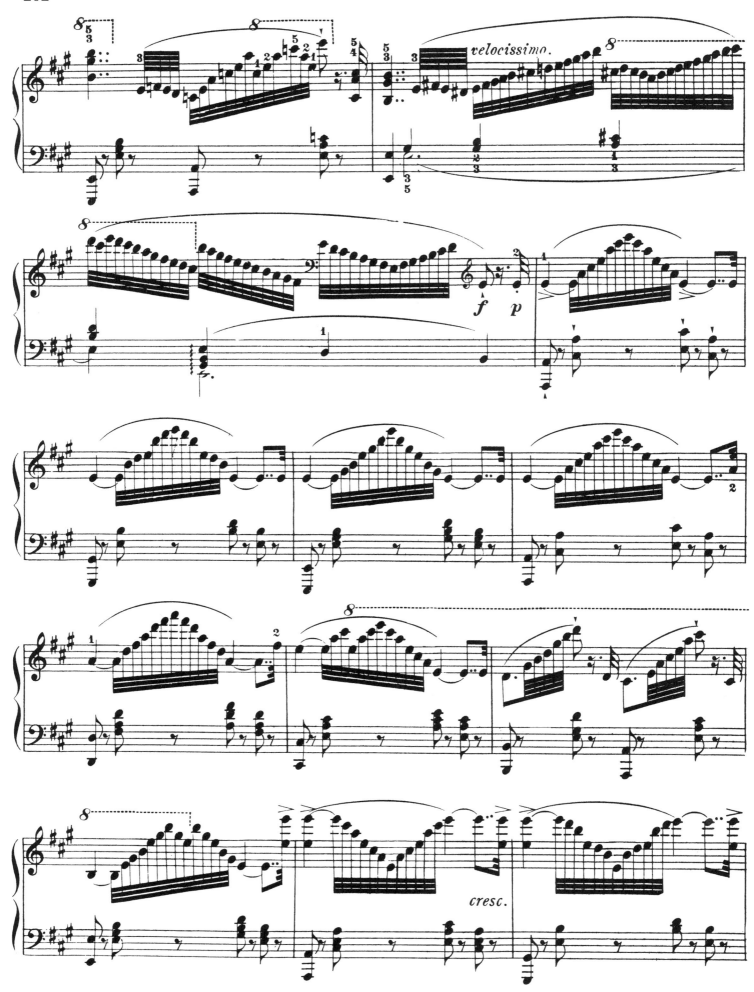

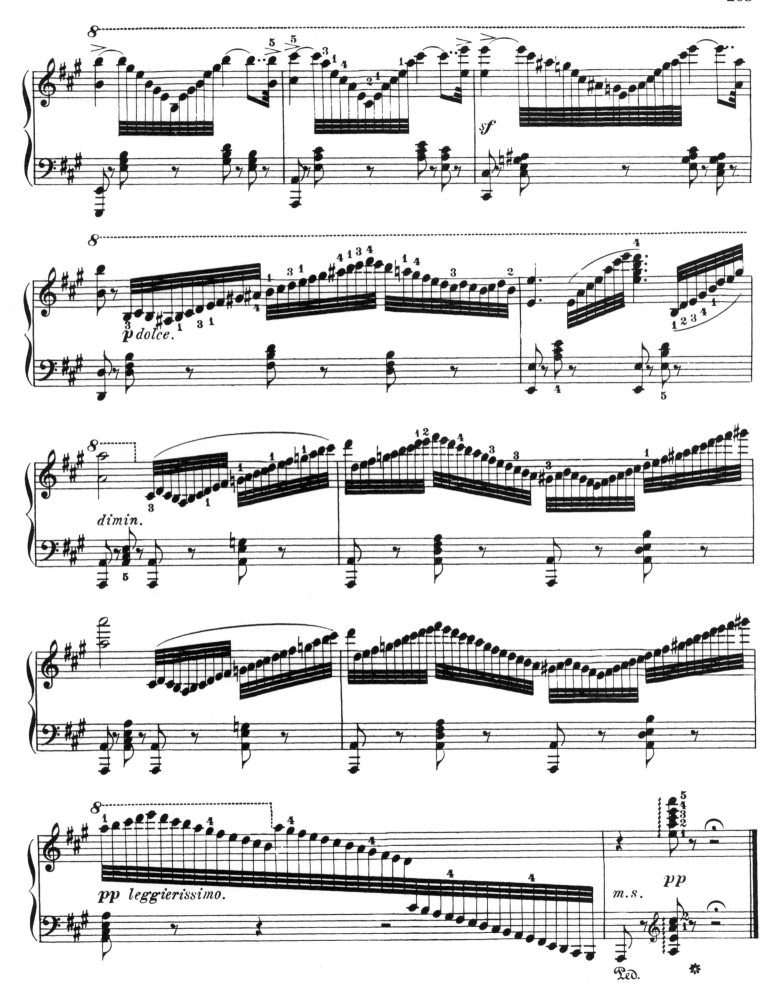

27.

Independence of the Fingers.

28.

A quiet Hand, the Fingers active to the utmost.

Allegro vivace. ($\quarternote$ = 144)

29.

Mordent-Exercise.

30.

To acquire a firm Touch.

This Study must, at first, be practiced in the following way:

Vivace. ($\quad = 126$)

31.

Practice in the Passing under of the Thumb.

32.

Uniformity in raising the Fingers.

THE ART OF FINGER DEXTERITY
Op. 740, Book 5

Revised and fingered by
Max Vogrich

Carl Czerny
(1791–1857)

33.

Octave Skips, the Hand light.

34.

Trills in Thirds.

35.

Changing the Fingers on one and the same Key.

36.

Light Arm, the Fingers flexible.

236

37.

Clearness in great Strength.

38.

Uniformity in raising the Hands.

39.

Exercise in Thirds.

40.

Light Breaking off or Detaching of Chords.

41.

Action of the Fingers of the Left Hand.

THE ART OF FINGER DEXTERITY
Op. 740, Book 6

Revised and fingered by
Max Vogrich

42.

Carl Czerny
(1791–1857)

Double-Mordent-Exercise.

43.

Skill in the Passing under of the Thumb.

44.

The lightest Touch, the Fingers exerted to the utmost.

45.

Legato Melody with broken Chords.

46.

Bravura in Touch and Action.

47.

Delicate and distinct Touch in broken Chords.

Molto allegro. (♩ = 92)

48.
Triller-Uebung.
(Trill-Exercise.)

Allegro commodo. ($\quad$ = 116)

49.

Octaves Bravura.

277

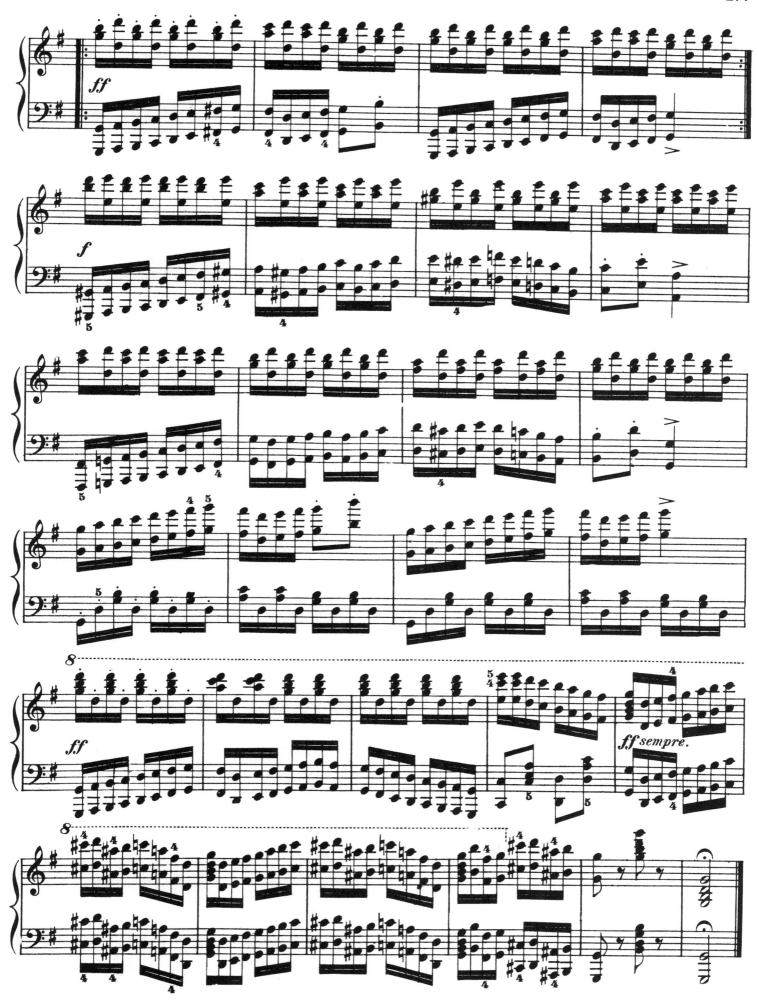

50.

Bravura in Touch and Tempo.

THIRTY NEW STUDIES IN TECHNICS
Op. 849, Book 1

Carl Czerny
(1791–1857)

+) Also practice this study transposed a semitone higher.

+) It is a good plan also to transpose this exercise a semitone higher, adhering to the same fingering.

THIRTY NEW STUDIES IN TECHNICS
Op. 849, Book 2

Carl Czerny
(1791–1857)

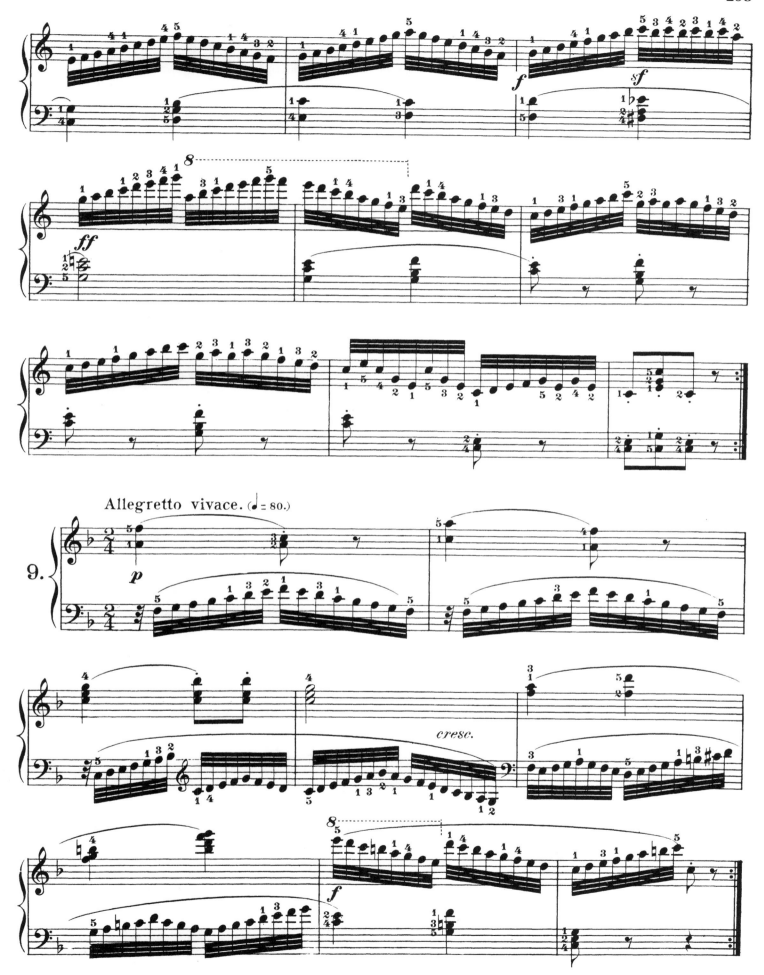

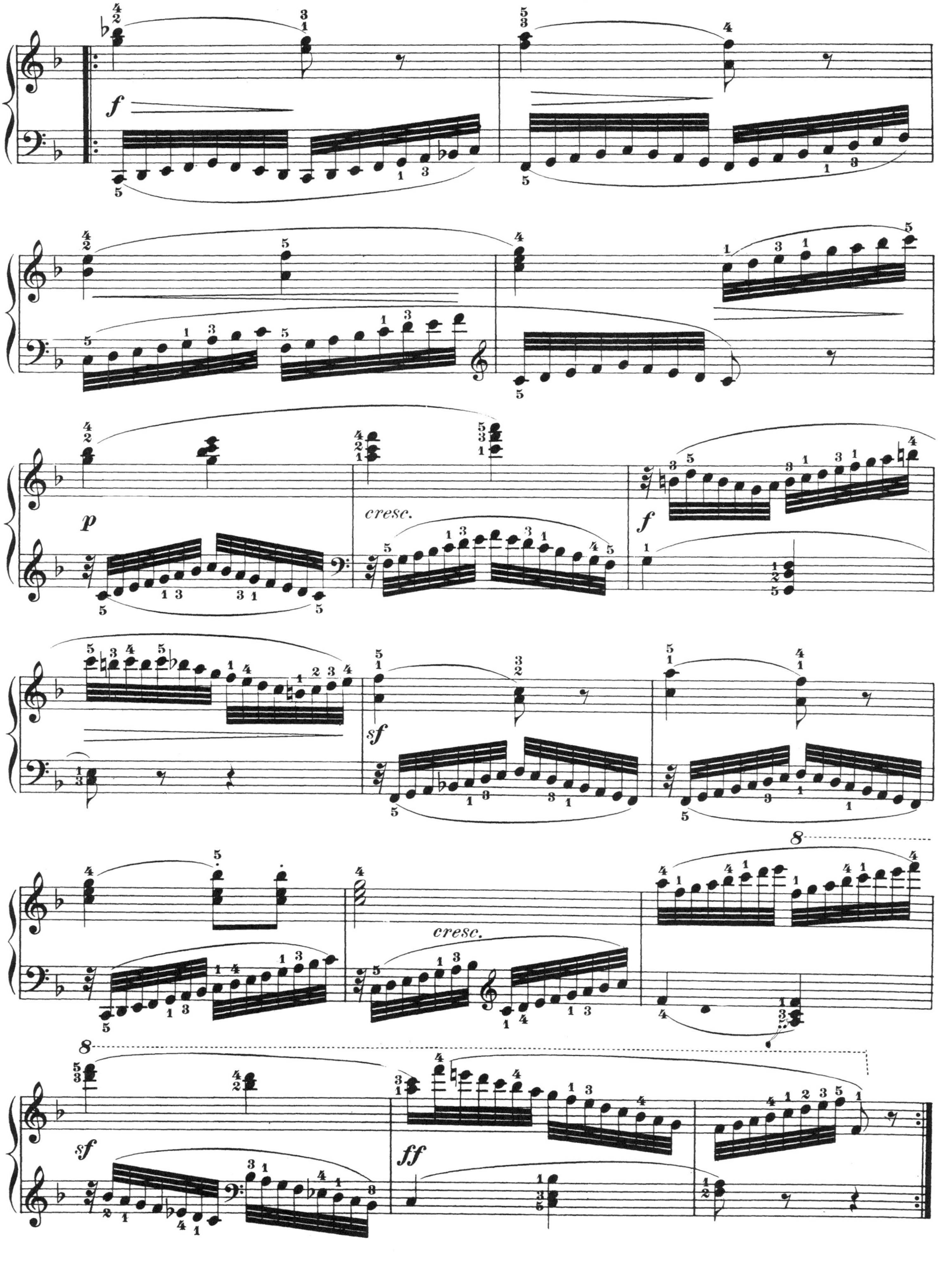
f
p
cresc.
f
sf
cresc.
8
8
sf
ff

*) Also practice in F♯.

298

THIRTY NEW STUDIES IN TECHNICS

Op. 849, Book 3

Carl Czerny
(1791–1857)

✛) Also practice in Gb, making only indispensable changes in the fingering.

Molto vivace e leggiero.(♩. = 96.)

13.

THIRTY NEW STUDIES IN TECHNICS
Op. 849, Book 4

Carl Czerny
(1791–1857)

✝) Also transpose into C♯ and C♭, retaining the fingering given.

THIRTY NEW STUDIES IN TECHNICS
Op. 849, Book 5

Carl Czerny
(1791–1857)

Allegro comodo. (♩ = 132.)

23.

p legato.

cresc.

f

f

sf

p

324

THIRTY NEW STUDIES IN TECHNICS

Op. 849, Book 6

Carl Czerny
(1791–1857)

+)Also practice in D♭, making the necessary changes in the fingering, particularly in measures **7** and **17**.

328

26.